This special gift is for: _____

From: _____

By His Grace
My Journey Was Revealed

Affirmations of a Soul in Recovery

Valecia A. Baldwin-Johnson

Order this book online at www.trafford.com
or email orders@trafford.com

Most Trafford titles are also available at major online book retailers.

Print information available on the last page.

ISBN: 978-1-4120-5836-0 (sc)

Trafford rev. 07/27/2015

Trafford PUBLISHING www.trafford.com
North America & international
toll-free: 1 888 232 4444 (USA & Canada)
fax: 812 355 4082

By His Grace
My Journey Was Revealed
Valecia A. Baldwin-Johnson
Affirmations of a Soul In Recovery

It is my hope that many people around the world will read the words of this book and profoundly understand they are not alone. They are not alone in their experiences, thoughts, feelings, and desires.

It is not enough to talk about coming from a dysfunctional family or being aware of dysfunctional behaviors that shape our lives. The challenge of living is to recognize that all of the experiences we have shared can be the foundation for a sometimes difficult but rewarding Journey.

You are not alone! Dare to embrace life's challenges and see what miracles are revealed. Are you ready to live life today and embrace the Journey?

I dedicate this book to all of the peole I have met along my journey. I realize there are no mistakes in life. My journey has not been easy but it has been a wonderful Blessing!

A special thank you to my family for their love and support throughout the years. I am especially grateful to my children for loving me in such an unconditional manner. To my three year old son Juliyen: you have no idea how you have taught me to laugh out loud everyday and sometimes even at myself. To my twenty-one year old daughter Brandi, your forgiving spirit has taught me to exhibit love with gentleness. Thank you for "saving" me from myself. Your love has lifted me many, many times over.

I will laugh out loud everyday!

I am worthy because
I live, I breathe, I see,
I am... it is my right!

Life is manageable.

Today, I celebrate the ability to feel.

I will take better care
of myself.

I can protect myself from the "Boogeyman."

I will no longer feel
guilty when I have
happy experiences.

I deserve happiness!

I can genuinely smile
knowing others will
welcome my warmth.

I am learning to break the cycle of unhealthy living and loving.

I am not responsible for the pain and suffering that existed within my family.

I will learn from the
addictive behaviors I
witnessed as a child.

I am a Champion!

I can share myself with others knowing that isolation is not healthy.

I no longer need to "buy" friends.

Although, I am learning to forgive enormous pain still exists.

I can trust others.

Others can trust me.

I can depend on
family and friends to
help me through the
tough times.

It is okay to fail...
but I am never a
failure.

I can embrace others with love.

Everyone is not the enemy!

The world is not out to "get" me.

I will no longer sabotage my happiness.

I will not allow others to sabotage my happiness.

I am not afraid of
"quiet" time.

I will no longer manipulate situations to gain acceptance and approval.

I no longer need to be the best at everything to be okay.

I give myself permission to rest when I am tired.

It is okay to admit that I am tired.

I have a right to my opinion.

My opinion matters.

I have a right to say no.

I will consider the opinion of others.

I will cherish my worth by limiting how much I give away.

Violence is never okay!

I will no longer
confuse physical
abuse for love.

I am worthy of attracting honest people in my life.

I am worthy of keeping honest people in my life.

I will give less when I have less.

I will give more when
I have more.

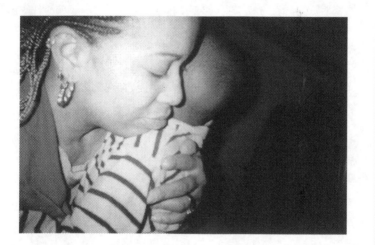

I will not cry in
secret.

It is okay to appear fragile and weak at times.

I can face my demons
without exploiting
the weaknesses of
others.

I am no longer falling from windows in my dreams.

I am sorry for intentionally hurting others.

I can wear uncoordinated clothing and still be worthy.

I am greater than my clothing.

I can live life spontaneously and survive.

I will say thank you and please more often.

I can unleash my childhood fears and begin to trust.

It has never been my responsibility to "heal" family members.

It has never been my responsibility to "save" family members.

I can protect
myself from hurtful
individuals.

I can sleep without having nightmares.

I am greater than my history.

I am greater than my family's history.

I was not born to be rejected.

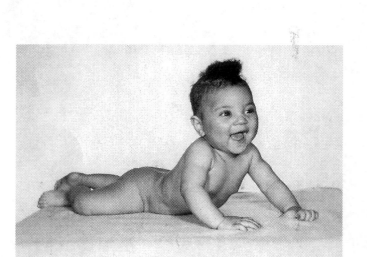

I have developed a
safe sense of identity.

I apologize for attacking others by using foul language.

I am continuing to
work on exhibiting
patience and grace.

My broken heart will heal.

I can see TRUTH.

I want to see
TRUTH.

I speak truth because
I am no longer
afraid.

I speak, seek and see truth where it exists.

I am no longer haunted in my sleep.

I am no longer attracted to individuals who want to use me.

I will not let my
SPIRIT be broken.

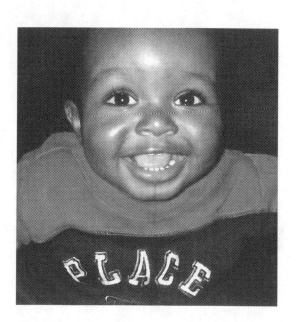

I am an alcoholic by birth.

I will be in
RECOVERY for the
rest of my life.

I am a drug addict through marriage.

I will be in
RECOVERY for the
rest of my life.

I take responsibility
for my actions ...
past, present, and
those to come!

Fear kept me hostage
in my relationships
but now I am free.

I do not have all the answers.

I look forward to sharing myself with others.

I will speak
openly about my
experiences.

It is okay to be lonely.

It is okay to be alone at times.

I will require honesty in my relationships.

I will continue to
write the rules for
my healthy living.

I will not be
mistreated.

I will not mistreat others.

I am able to tell others that I love them and really mean it.

I will not be ignored.

I will maintain direct eye contact when speaking.

I will not make
excuses for the bad
behavior of others.

I will not make excuses for others – PERIOD!

I will begin to love
myself today.

I love myslef just the way I am.

"Truth" can be
painful but I realize
it is necessary.

I will seek out healthy, nurturing relationships.

I am worthy of attracting people with integrity in my life.

I am worthy of keeping people with integrity in my life.

I can deviate from
my plans and still
have fun.

I can rest in peace.

I look forward to
meeting new people.

Survival is not
an option. It is a
requirement for
better living.

I will create a voice
that speaks volumes
about me.

I feel alive.

I am alive.

I am "Born Again."

I can achieve all great things.

Happiness begins
and ends with me.

Life is Great!

Life is Grand!

Yesterday was a BLESSING!

I am not afraid of TOMORROW!

I look forward to TODAY!

My journey is just beginning!

By His Grace –
I accept my Recovery!

Printed in the United States
By Bookmasters